Original title:
Dreams of Magic

Author: Atticus Thornton

ISBN HARDBACK: 978-9916-90-608-8
ISBN PAPERBACK: 978-9916-90-609-5

Riddles of the Starlit Sky

Whispers of night tell tales so bright,
Stars woven in a shimmering light.
Questions linger in the cosmic dance,
Each twinkle a chance, a fleeting glance.

Mysterious orbs with stories to share,
Guardians of secrets floating in air.
What lies beyond their glittering gaze?
A realm of dreams in celestial haze.

Fading flashes in the heavens above,
Riddles abound, wrapped in love.
What connects the dots in the dark?
Patterns unfolding, igniting a spark.

In the silence, the universe sighs,
Answering softly, as time flits and flies.
Enigmas hidden in the night's cloak,
Unraveling truths in each star's smoke.

Constellations of Enchantment

Under starlight, stories unfold,
Constellations of magic, bold.
Mythical figures traced with care,
In the vast expanse, dreams take air.

A bear, a warrior, a maiden in flight,
Each telling tales in the quiet night.
Mapping legends in the sky's embrace,
A journey of wonder, in time and space.

Twinkling diamonds in the velvet blue,
Gaze upon wonders that feel so true.
Where do the lost hearts find their way?
Guided by light till the break of day.

With every glance, we weave our fate,
In the art of the cosmos, we create.
From ancient lore to whispers of now,
Constellations of enchantment, take a bow.

Realms Beyond the Veil

In shadows deep where spirits roam,
Whispers call to a distant home.
Through misty pathways, secrets glide,
In realms where lost souls often hide.

Stars above, a guiding hand,
Illuminate this haunted land.
With every step, the echoes swell,
To realms beyond the darkened veil.

Chronicles of the Wandering Light

Across the darkened skies it sweeps,
A flicker where the silence weeps.
In uncharted spaces, it takes flight,
A tale of dreams in the tranquil night.

Casting hope on the weary ground,
In moments lost, serenity found.
Through trials faced and shadows fought,
The wandering light brings peace, unbought.

Glimmering Echoes of Infinity

In timeless waves where stars unite,
Echoes dance, bathed in pure light.
Each shimmer holds a whispered tale,
Of worlds unseen beyond the pale.

In every gleam, a destiny waits,
Endless wonders, open gates.
To grasp the dreams that seek to fly,
In glimmering echoes, hearts comply.

The Illusionary Nook

In a corner where shadows fade,
Lies a realm that dreams have made.
With colors bright, they twist and bend,
A sanctuary where time won't end.

The walls whisper secrets of the past,
In this nook, memories cast.
A fleeting glimpse, a fleeting touch,
In illusion's realm, we crave so much.

Whimsy in the Twilight

As day surrenders to the night,
The stars above begin to light.
Whispers dance on gentle breeze,
In twilight's charm, the heart finds ease.

Dancing shadows play around,
In this soft glow, dreams abound.
Each flicker tells a timeless tale,
Where magic lingers, not to pale.

Crickets serenade the moon,
Their symphony, a soft cocoon.
With laughter wrapped in evening's grace,
Life's wonder hides in twilight's embrace.

In every twinkle, a wish to chase,
In every sigh, a warm embrace.
Through whimsical winds, we find our way,
In twilight's arms, we'll forever stay.

Chasing the Aurora

In polar skies, the colors blend,
A cosmic dance that won’t soon end.
Shimmering lights begin to soar,
Igniting hearts, we yearn for more.

We chase the hues of green and gold,
Each ribbon of light, a story told.
Underneath this glowing scene,
Our dreams are woven, bright and keen.

With every gasp, the night ignites,
In nature’s art, we find delights.
Each heartbeat syncs with nature’s song,
In the aurora, we feel we belong.

Together, we embrace the night,
Guided by this breathtaking sight.
In chasing dreams beneath the stars,
We find our path, no matter how far.

A Cauldron of Tidal Dreams

Where ocean whispers kiss the shore,
A cauldron brews of tales galore.
Each wave a story, deep and vast,
In the ebb and flow, the die is cast.

Moonlit dances stir the sea,
A rhythm that sets our spirits free.
With hands outstretched, we catch the tide,
In watery depths, our dreams reside.

Flavors of salt and breeze entwine,
In every ripple, messages divine.
We sail on hopes, our sails unfurled,
In the cauldron's charm, we find our world.

A harmony of waves and dreams,
In this vast realm, everything gleams.
With every crest, our hearts take flight,
In a cauldron of dreams, we find our light.

Synchronicity in Shadows

In fleeting moments, time aligns,
When chance encounters weave the signs.
Echoes dance in dim-lit night,
In shadows' grasp, we find our light.

A shared glance ignites the spark,
Awakening magic in the dark.
With whispered secrets on the breeze,
The world conspires to tease and please.

From silent wishes to subtle truths,
Life reveals its playful roots.
Through tangled paths, we roam and sway,
In synchronicity, we find our way.

Every shadow holds a thread,
Connecting hearts with words unsaid.
In this tapestry, we create,
A dance of fate, we celebrate.

Whispers of Enchanted Slumber

Softly hum the dreams of night,
Guiding stars with tender light.
In shadows deep, the wishes flow,
To realms where only dreamers go.

Crickets sing their lullaby,
As clouds drift in the velvet sky.
Each sigh a secret, softly shared,
In slumber's arms, we dream, prepared.

Misty visions, glowing bright,
Dance within the heart's delight.
Enchanted whispers call us near,
In quiet moments, love draws near.

Embrace the peace, let worries fade,
In twilight's arms, our dreams cascade.
Whispers of slumber beckon slow,
A world of magic, soft and low.

Lullabies of Stardust Hearts

Cradled in the night so clear,
Lullabies drift, sweet and dear.
Stardust shines in gentle streams,
Filling up our tender dreams.

Hearts alight with cosmic grace,
Dancing through the endless space.
Moonlit melodies softly play,
Guiding us till break of day.

In whispers soft, the universe,
Spins tales of love in gentle verse.
Every note a starry spark,
Illuminating dreams in dark.

With every breath, the cosmos sighs,
As we weave our lullabies.
Stardust hearts, forever bright,
Embrace the magic of the night.

Fantasies Woven in Moonlight

In moonlit skies, the dreams take flight,
Weaving softly through the night.
Magic threads in silver spins,
As the dance of wonder begins.

Every twinkle tells a tale,
Of whispered wishes on the trail.
Fantasies lost in twilight's glow,
Where secret rivers gently flow.

With each heartbeat, time stands still,
Echoes of dreams fulfill the thrill.
In shadows deep, the visions rise,
Bright reflections in our eyes.

Moonlight’s touch, a sweet caress,
Guiding us through wilderness.
In every heart, the dreams reside,
Fantasies woven, side by side.

Enigma of the Celestial Veil

Behind the veil of twinkling skies,
Lies an enigma that never dies.
Stars whisper secrets, old yet new,
In celestial dances, forever true.

Nebulas swirl with colors bright,
Painting the canvas of the night.
In cosmic realms, we seek the key,
Unlocking wonders for all to see.

A galaxy of dreams unfurls,
As mysteries of the cosmos twirl.
With each heartbeat, beyond the pale,
We find ourselves, the sought-after trail.

The heavens hum a timeless song,
Where every soul knows it belongs.
In the embrace of night's delight,
The enigma blooms, a guiding light.

Astral Journeys in Slumber

In the quiet of the night,
Stars whisper and take flight.
Dreams weave through cosmic trails,
Lost in the mystic veils.

Moonlit paths guide my way,
To realms where the stardust play.
Visions dance, colors collide,
In this magical astral ride.

Floating through ethereal tides,
Where time and space abides.
Moments stretch and bend like light,
In the arms of endless night.

As dawn creeps with gentle grace,
I awaken from this embrace.
Yet the whispers linger near,
In the dreams I hold so dear.

Magic in the Morning Mist

Morning breaks with softest glow,
Mist envelops earth below.
Every leaf and petal gleams,
In the light of waking dreams.

Whispers of the dawn arise,
Painting colors in the skies.
Nature's breath, a sacred hymn,
Awakens wonder on a whim.

Fantasy in every drop,
As the world begins to hop.
Magic lingers in the air,
Inviting hearts to feel and care.

In each shimmer, secrets lie,
Promises of joy, oh my.
A tapestry of life unfolds,
Wrapped in warmth, a tale retold.

The Dance of Faery Lights

In the woods where shadows creep,
Faery lights begin to leap.
Twinkling like stars in the night,
They twirl in gleeful, frolic flight.

Whispers soft as the night air,
Calling dreamers unaware.
Each flicker a tale to narrate,
Of magic woven by fate.

Moonlit paths beneath the trees,
Guide the hearts that dare to believe.
Every step, a secret shared,
In this realm where few have dared.

Dancing with the fireflies,
Catching glimpses of the skies.
In this dance, all fears dissolve,
In a world where dreams revolve.

Nightflowers in a Dreamscape

In the garden of the night,
Flowers bloom in soft moonlight.
Petals glisten, softly sigh,
In dreams, where wishes lie.

Each blossom tells a story true,
Of hidden worlds just waiting for you.
Fragrant whispers fill the air,
Hopes and dreams within their care.

Dreamscape blooms beneath the stars,
Carrying secrets from afar.
Petals lace the blanket of earth,
Celebrating the magic of birth.

In this realm of shadowed grace,
Nightflowers weave a gentle trace.
Each moment, a fleeting kiss,
In the dreams we dare to miss.

A Twilight Woven Tale

As dusk descends on weary skies,
Whispers dance where shadows lie.
Dreams entwined in twilight's grace,
A tapestry of night we trace.

Echoes of the day now fade,
Stars awaken, gently played.
In this realm of softest light,
Hearts embrace the coming night.

The moon, a guardian on high,
Guides our thoughts as night birds fly.
Stories woven, both old and new,
A twilight tale, serene and true.

In the glow of stars aglow,
Let our secrets gently flow.
Each moment cherished, soft and frail,
In this twilight woven tale.

Fables Wreathed in Stars

Underneath the vast expanse,
Fables stir in quiet dance.
Stars alight with tales of lore,
Ancient whispers on the shore.

Each twinkle holds a story bright,
Of dreamers lost in worlds of night.
Wreathed in stardust, we take flight,
Chasing visions, pure delight.

Legends born in cosmic sighs,
Echo through the endless skies.
Secrets linger, soft and sweet,
In every tale where starlight meets.

With every gaze, our hearts ignite,
Fables woven, full of light.
In the heavens, truths unfurl,
Wreathed in stars, our timeless world.

The Ethereal Silhouette

In moonlit shadows, figures sway,
An ethereal dance at close of day.
Silhouettes of dreams take flight,
Caught within the fabric of night.

Glimmers softly touch the ground,
As whispers weave a magic sound.
Each moment drawn in silence sweet,
An artist's brush, the night a sheet.

A reflection of what may be,
Inneath the stars, we find the key.
Silhouettes of hopes and fears,
Crafted gently through the years.

With every stroke the heart reveals,
An artful echo, love unveils.
In shadows deep, let spirits glow,
The ethereal silhouette we know.

Threads of Stardust

In the weave of night, we find,
Threads of stardust, intertwined.
Gold and silver softly gleam,
Binding every whispered dream.

Woven tightly, fate's embrace,
Shimmering strands in cosmic space.
Each thread tells a tale of grace,
In the tapestry, we trace.

Crafted by the hands of time,
Every moment, every rhyme.
Strings of light in harmony,
Craft a song of destiny.

Through the fabric of our days,
Threads of stardust guide our ways.
In the cosmos, let us trust,
In the weave of dreams, we must.

Waking the Ethereal

In the realm where shadows sigh,
Dreams unfold like whispered sighs.
Chasing echoes, spirits roam,
Awakening in twilight's dome.

Stars igniting in the night,
Painting worlds with silver light.
Gentle whispers, secrets call,
Waking magic in us all.

Softly drifting through the haze,
Lost in time’s enchanted maze.
Veils of mist begin to part,
Revealing wonders of the heart.

As dawn breaks with golden rays,
Ethereal dance that truly sways.
In this moment, we arise,
Embracing life, a sweet surprise.

Fantasies on a Silver Canvas

Brush of dreams in twilight’s hand,
A silver canvas, visions grand.
Colors swirling, shadows blend,
On this art, our hearts depend.

Whispers of a nightingale,
Chasing starlight on the trail.
Each stroke tells a story bright,
Tales of hope and endless flight.

Laughter echoes in the glow,
Fleeting moments, soft and slow.
In the dreamer's secret space,
Fantasies find a warm embrace.

Layer upon layer, we create,
Binding fate with strokes of fate.
In this realm of vibrant hues,
We paint the world, our hopes renew.

The Illusionist’s Cradle

In a cradle of twilight dreams,
Magic dances in silver beams.
Fingers weave through whispered spells,
Where the heart of wonder dwells.

Shadows shift and colors blend,
Imagination knows no end.
What is real, what’s just a game?
In this world, it's all the same.

With a flick, illusions form,
Chasing shadows, breaking norm.
Every trick a tale untold,
In the night, the magic bold.

Laughter echoes near and far,
As we reach for every star.
In the cradle, let them play,
Illusions guide us on our way.

Secrets of the Twilight Realm

Hidden deep where shadows swell,
Twilight whispers secrets swell.
Ancient trees with roots that sigh,
Guarding tales of days gone by.

Moonlit paths and stardust trails,
In this world, adventure pales.
Creatures dance with grace divine,
In the twilight, all align.

Silence wraps the evening tight,
Softly cradling the night.
In the heart of this timeless space,
Secrets bloom, a sacred place.

Every glance holds magic's spark,
In the realm where dreams embark.
Twilight's cloak, so softly sewn,
Unraveling the unknown.

Invoking the Midnight Muse

In shadows deep, where silence sighs,
A whisper stirs, as darkness flies.
The stars align, a canvas pure,
Awakening dreams, so bright, so sure.

With pen in hand, the worlds unfold,
Mysteries wrapped in twilight's gold.
Each stroke a dance, each thought a flame,
Invoking wonders, none can tame.

The moonlight weaves through branches bare,
Casting spells upon the air.
A muse, she beckons, soft and sweet,
In midnight's grasp, our hearts shall meet.

As dawn approaches, shadows blend,
A fleeting hour, we cannot fend.
Yet in this night, our spirits bloom,
In secret paths, we chase the moon.

The Harmony of Enchantment

In whispers low, the night takes flight,
A symphony, the stars ignite.
With every note, the world aligns,
In harmony, the magic shines.

The breeze, it carries tales untold,
Of ancient myths and hearts of gold.
As fireflies dance, they paint the sky,
In this enchanted night, we fly.

With every heartbeat, rhythms blend,
Nature's magic, a timeless friend.
In shadows deep, we find the tune,
A song of love beneath the moon.

Awake, arise, let spirits soar,
In melodies, we crave for more.
The harmony, forever plays,
In whispered dreams, we lose our ways.

Tales from the Celestial Grove

In celestial grove, the stars do hum,
With gentle grace, the night has come.
Beneath the boughs, old stories weave,
In every breath, the night will leave.

Soft rustling leaves, a tale begins,
Of earthly woes and fairy wins.
Around the fire, shadows dance,
In sacred space, we lose our chance.

With whispered secrets, the skies unfold,
Each twinkling light, a dream retold.
The owls will hoot, and crickets sing,
In this paradise, our hearts take wing.

So gather close, let legends flow,
In every heart, the magic grows.
Among the stars, we paint our dreams,
In celestial glow, forever gleams.

Secrets in the Moon's Embrace

In silver beams, the secrets lie,
In moon's soft glow, we learn to fly.
The night conceals what day won't see,
In shadows deep, we long to be.

With every glance, the whispers grew,
Of ancient paths, and skies so blue.
In moonlit dances, hearts collide,
Where time stands still, and dreams abide.

The world asleep, but spirits wake,
To share the tales that dreams can make.
In every sigh, love's promise glows,
In moon's embrace, our mystery flows.

As dawn approaches, the secrets fade,
Yet in our hearts, the feelings stayed.
In echoes soft, the night remains,
In memories wrapped in moonlit chains.

Shimmering Veils of Night

The stars flicker softly, bright,
Casting shadows in the light,
Whispers of dreams take their flight,
Beneath the shimmering veils of night.

Clouds drift like ghosts on the breeze,
Wrapped in secrets, they tease,
With every rustle of leaves,
Nature's symphony never flees.

The moon, a guardian high,
Watches over as we sigh,
In this moment, hearts comply,
To the magic woven in the sky.

Time slows in this gentle embrace,
Every worry finds its place,
In the stillness, we find grace,
In shimmering veils, we softly trace.

The Curiosity of the Moon's Gaze

The moon hangs low, full and round,
Casting dreams upon the ground,
A curious light, so profound,
In the night, whispers abound.

She watches lovers dance so close,
Witness to what none may expose,
With every gaze, she interpose,
Secrets shared, where passion grows.

The shadows stretch in her glow,
Where hope and longing gently flow,
Each silver beam, a silent show,
Of tales untold, yet to bestow.

In the stillness, questions rise,
Reflecting truth in hidden sighs,
In the moon's gaze, wisdom lies,
A gentle heart that never denies.

Tides of the Enchanted Sea

Waves crash gently on the shore,
Whispers of secrets, tales of yore,
The ocean sings, a mighty roar,
Tides of magic evermore.

Under the surface, dreams reside,
In the depths where hopes abide,
With every ebb, stories glide,
Mysteries the sea won't hide.

Seagulls dance on ocean's breeze,
Guided by waves with perfect ease,
In this realm, the heart finds peace,
Tides beckon, encouraging release.

The sun dips low, painting the skies,
Reflecting journeys, timeless ties,
In the enchanted sea, we rise,
Embracing wonders, as the heart flies.

The Lantern’s Lull

A lantern glows, soft and warm,
In the night, it calms the storm,
Casting light where shadows form,
In its embrace, we find our charm.

The flicker tells a tale anew,
Of paths we tread, of morning dew,
A guiding star, forever true,
In the darkness, it breaks through.

Its light draws close the weary heart,
In each flicker, life’s fresh start,
In quiet moments, we partake,
A lantern's lull, a gentle wake.

Together we sit, hand in hand,
In the glow, we understand,
With every flicker, dreams expand,
In the lantern’s lull, we make our stand.

The Alchemy of Nightfall

The sun dips low behind the hills,
Shadows stretch, the quiet stills.
Stars awaken in velvet skies,
Painting dreams as daylight sighs.

Whispers breeze through ancient trees,
Carrying secrets on the breeze.
The moon ignites a silver glow,
Transforming worlds with every flow.

In night's embrace, we softly drift,
Finding solace, a gentle gift.
Magic lingers, softly spun,
Where all beginnings meet their run.

In alchemies of dusk and dawn,
We paint our dreams until they're gone.
Each heartbeat hums a timeless tune,
Beneath the watchful eye of the moon.

Mirages of a Fairytale Mind

In visions spun from dreams untold,
A tapestry of tales unfolds.
Castles rise on clouds so fair,
Where wishes dance in fragrant air.

Wanderers seek with hopeful hearts,
Through realms where each adventure starts.
Magic echoes in every sound,
Where joy and wonder can be found.

Dragons soar on whispering winds,
As laughter mingles, life begins.
In every mirage, a story gleams,
Awakening our wildest dreams.

Embrace the magic, let it flow,
For in this world, the heart must know.
That fairytales are never far,
They shine in us, our guiding star.

Moonbeams and Enchanted Flights

Underneath the silver glow,
Dreams take wing, and spirits flow.
With moonbeams bright, we sail the night,
Chasing shadows, hearts alight.

Luminous paths of stardust trail,
Where whispers of the cosmos sail.
Every glance a wish takes flight,
In the magic of the night.

Wings of hope on breezes soar,
Through realms unseen forevermore.
With every breath, we touch the sky,
Embraced by night, we learn to fly.

The world below fades from our sight,
As we embark on dreams so bright.
In every echo, freedom calls,
A journey where adventure sprawls.

The Sorcerer's Gentle Call

Through misty woods, a voice does weave,
An ancient spell that none perceive.
Softly beckoning the brave and wise,
With promises of hidden skies.

Each flicker, each spark of light,
Igniting dreams in the quiet night.
Enchantments dance upon the breeze,
Whispering secrets to the trees.

Hearts awaken to the sorcerer's art,
As magic flows, it stirs the heart.
With each incantation, shadows fall,
Revealing truths in the gentle call.

In twilight's grasp, we learn to hear,
The songs of magic drawing near.
Through tethered minds and souls so free,
The sorcerer's whispers guide you and me.

Enchanted Reveries Touched by Time

In twilight's embrace, the stars ignite,
Memories whisper, a soft delight.
Time weaves melodies, both sweet and rare,
Each moment a treasure, beyond compare.

Through corridors of dreams, we drift and sway,
Chasing the echoes of yesterday.
Golden leaves tumble, in crisp autumn air,
Every heartbeat sings, with beauty to share.

Beneath the silver moon, shadows play,
Infinite wonders in night's array.
A tapestry rich, in colors divine,
Enchanting our souls, with threads of time.

Labyrinth of Whimsy and Lore

In a garden where laughter blooms bright,
Whispers of secrets take joyous flight.
Pathways of curious twists and bends,
Where every corner, a story sends.

Wandering through the maze of delight,
Fairies dance beneath the soft moonlight.
Lost in the charm of the tales we weave,
In the labyrinth's heart, we dare to believe.

Jesters and jest, in colors so bold,
Each step revealing the magic untold.
With whimsy our guide, we venture and roam,
In this enchanted realm, we find our home.

The Dance of Forgotten Fantasies

In the hush of night, dreams take their flight,
Dances of shadows in ethereal light.
Whispers of longing brush softly the air,
Forgotten delights and wishes laid bare.

A waltz through the echoes of yesteryears,
Each twirl igniting both laughter and tears.
Fantasies flourish in twilight's embrace,
In the theater of stars, we find our place.

Memory's enigma, a tapestry spun,
Reality fades, as illusions outrun.
With each fleeting moment, the past intertwines,
In the dance of the heart, where love brightly shines.

Shadows of the Mystic Dawn

As dawn breaks softly, a new tale unfolds,
Whispers of hope in the silence it holds.
Shadows retreat, bowing to the day,
In the light's warm embrace, darkness gives way.

Reflections emerge on the glistening dew,
Colors awaken, in hues bright and true.
Mystic whispers ride on the gentle breeze,
Carrying promises, as the world starts to tease.

Among ancient trees, secrets convene,
The dawn's golden fingers, weaving the green.
With each rising sun, new dreams take their form,
In the shadows of morning, courage is born.

Wings of Illusion and Light

In shadows dance the whispers bright,
Where dreams take flight in silent night.
A canvas painted with skies so bold,
The secrets of the heart unfold.

With every flutter, hope ignites,
Chasing phantoms, chasing sights.
A symphony of stars above,
Guiding souls with wings of love.

Through portals spun of gleaming thread,
The stories linger, softly said.
In this realm where echoes play,
Illusions beckon, come what may.

And as the dawn breaks through the haze,
We journey forth in sunlit rays.
With wings unfurled, we rise and soar,
To chase the dreams forevermore.

Serenade of the Starlit Path

Beneath the gleam of silver night,
A path unfolds in dreams so bright.
With every step, the starlight glows,
In whispered tales that softly flows.

Each twinkle sings a soothing tune,
The night adorned with gentle moon.
As shadows sway in soft embrace,
We find our peace in this sweet space.

The universe in harmony,
A melody that sets us free.
With hearts aligned, we dance and sing,
To every hope that starlight brings.

And as we wander hand in hand,
Through this enchanted, timeless land.
The serenade lights up our way,
In peace we walk, till break of day.

Chronicles of the Hidden Realm

In realms unknown, the stories weave,
A tapestry of dreams to cleave.
With whispers caught in the twilight's edge,
Time unfolds a secret pledge.

Between the trees, the shadows hide,
Ancient spirits, a watchful guide.
They speak in rustles, warm and clear,
A language felt but seldom near.

Through every glance of glimmering light,
Mysteries dance, taking flight.
In echoes soft, the past remains,
In hidden realms, where magic reigns.

As twilight fades, the pages turn,
For every lesson, the heart will learn.
In chronicles vast, we find our way,
To hidden realms at end of day.

Visions in a Crystal Sphere

Within a sphere, reflections swirl,
A glimpse of futures, dreams unfurl.
Each vision shines, both bright and clear,
In this crystal world, we draw near.

A dance of colors, a glance of fate,
With every turn, we contemplate.
The mysteries held in fragile grace,
Invite us forth to seek this place.

As moments pause and time stands still,
We find in visions, strength and will.
Through crystal paths our spirits soar,
Unlocking truths forevermore.

With open hearts, we seek to see,
The stories wrapped in destiny.
In crystal spheres, we find our song,
Guided by the light all along.

Believe in the Uncharted Skies

In whispered winds, the journey starts,
A heart unbound, where wanderers chart.
Stars above, like dreams take flight,
Guiding souls through the endless night.

With every cloud, a secret lies,
Echoes of hope in uncharted skies.
Dare to tread where few have dared,
In the silence, the magic shared.

From valleys deep to mountains high,
The compass points to the open sky.
Believe in wonders yet to find,
Awakening the dreams entwined.

With courage fierce, and eyes aglow,
Embrace the path where few would go.
For in the chase, a truth resides,
In every doubt, the heart abides.

Mystical Glow of Distant Realms

Beyond the veil, where shadows dance,
The mystical glow sparks every glance.
Lights that flicker, colors blend,
In distant realms where dreams transcend.

Whispers of time in twilight's breath,
Unfolding tales of love and death.
Stars are stories, spun so bright,
Guiding hearts through the velvety night.

In hidden places, secrets swirl,
The glow ignites a timeless whirl.
Galaxies stretch, an endless sea,
Each spark a chance for you and me.

In this vastness, find your way,
Through echoes soft, where shadows play.
Embrace the unknown, let it gleam,
In the mystical glow, we dare to dream.

Echoing the Luminance of Dreams

In the echo of a quiet night,
Dreams awaken, filled with light.
A tapestry of whispered wishes,
Floating soft like moonlit fishes.

With every heartbeat, a vision clear,
The luminance calls, inviting near.
Paths unfurl with every sigh,
Leading souls where wonders lie.

In the dance of shadows and beams,
Chasing the echo of distant dreams.
Stars align in prescient grace,
Reflecting hope on every face.

Hold close the magic, let it sway,
In the embrace of night and day.
For in the echoes, find your song,
A luminance where we belong.

The Artistry of Cosmic Portals

Through cosmic portals, dreams take flight,
An artistry crafted in the night.
Waves of color, a seamless blend,
Infinite chances where worlds extend.

A brush of stars, a canvas wide,
Awakens journeys that softly glide.
Boundless wonders await the heart,
In the artistry, we all take part.

With every heartbeat, galaxies spin,
Open your heart, let the magic in.
Each stroke a path, each hue a guide,
Through cosmic realms, together we ride.

In the tapestry woven, dreams align,
Portals of wonder, where stars will shine.
Embrace the beauty of all that’s near,
In the artistry of space, we disappear.

Celestial Whispers in the Void

Stars twinkle in the night,
Echoes from a distant light.
Galaxies in silent dance,
Mysteries of fate and chance.

Comets streak across the sky,
Wonders that make time comply.
In the dark, a voice we hear,
Guiding us without fear.

Planets spin on paths unseen,
Each a world, a vibrant dream.
Whispers of the cosmic sea,
Calling us to wander free.

In the void, silence reigns,
Yet in hearts, the starlight gains.
Celestial realms weave their thread,
In whispers of the sky, we're led.

A Song of Otherworldly Encounters

Beneath the moon's ethereal glow,
Strange shapes in shadows flow.
Voices dance on misty air,
Haunting melodies everywhere.

Through the night, the spirits roam,
Guiding lost souls back to home.
Songs of old fill the still night,
Chants that shimmer, pure delight.

From the depths, a soft refrain,
Echoing the joys and pain.
Every note, a bridge to time,
Carving dreams in verse and rhyme.

In the twilight, we connect,
To the unseen, we reflect.
These encounters shape our fate,
A cosmic tune, we celebrate.

The Spellbound Canvas of Night

Canvas dark, with sparkles bright,
Painting tales of day and night.
Every star, a brushstroke wide,
Creating worlds where dreams abide.

Nebulas swirl in colors bold,
Stories of the ancients told.
In the quiet, visions rise,
Woven threads of ancient skies.

Constellations weave their lore,
Mapping journeys to explore.
Each twinkle, a magical spark,
Illuminating paths through dark.

In the spellbound night we stand,
Mysteries at our command.
Let the cosmos be our guide,
In this canvas, we confide.

When the Unseen Comes Alive

Whispers of the night arise,
In the shadows, truth belies.
Hidden realms breathe and sigh,
Magic stirs as spirits fly.

When the clock strikes midnight's chime,
Time unfurls in mystic rhyme.
Ethereal figures twist and swirl,
In a dance, their secrets twirl.

Veils are thin, the air ignites,
With flickering ghostly lights.
In the silence, hearts collide,
Fearless in the dreamers' tide.

When the unseen comes alive,
With each pulse, we learn to thrive.
In the night, we find our place,
In the magic of embrace.

Secrets of the Twilight Realm

In shadows deep, where whispers dwell,
The twilight sings its mystic spell.
Stars are born, and fade away,
As dreams outlast the light of day.

The moonlight dances on silver streams,
Unearthing long-forgotten dreams.
With every sigh, the night unfolds,
Revealing secrets, softly told.

A borrower of dusk's embrace,
The twilight holds a secret place.
Where echoes linger, time stands still,
And hearts retreat to find their will.

In every shadow, stories brewed,
In twilight's hush, old hopes renewed.
Through veils of night, we glimpse the gleam,
Of whispered truths, a fleeting dream.

Ethereal Journeys Beyond the Veil

Step lightly through the silken mist,
Where realms collide and dreams persist.
Beyond the veil, in twilight's glow,
Lies a path that few may know.

With every step, the silence breathes,
A tapestry of fate it weaves.
Ethereal whispers guide the way,
To distant lands where shadows play.

In realms of wonder, time is lost,
Where every heart must count the cost.
A dance of light, a spark divine,
Awaits the brave who cross the line.

Boundless skies and jeweled seas,
In every moment, magic flees.
Ethereal journeys, tales unspun,
Awaiting those who dare to run.

A Tapestry of Myth and Wonder

Threads of gold and shades of night,
We weave a tale, a wondrous sight.
In every stitch, a legend glows,
A tapestry the cosmos knows.

From ancient seas to mountain peaks,
In whispered winds, the wisdom speaks.
Mythic beasts and heroes bold,
In every heart, their tales unfold.

With each new dawn, the stories rise,
Beneath the vast and endless skies.
In every heartbeat, magic sways,
A tapestry of endless days.

Legends dance on the edge of time,
In rhymes of fate, and reasoned rhyme.
We weave together dreams untold,
A tapestry of life, of gold.

Echoes of a Fabled Night

In fabled night where shadows creep,
Echoes stir beneath the deep.
In every sigh, a tale resides,
Of whispered dreams and hidden guides.

The stars align in memory's thread,
Where ancient songs of love are spread.
Fables wrapped in night's embrace,
Illuminate the hidden space.

From ages past, the stories call,
Their haunting tones, a siren's thrall.
In every echo, wisdom speaks,
Of joy and sorrow, strength and weak.

Awakened hearts, the night bestows,
A dance of dreams, a world that glows.
In echoes bright, we find our way,
Through fabled night to break of day.

Enchanted Reflections on Still Waters

In twilight's glow, the waters gleam,
Mirroring dreams, a breath, a stream.
Soft whispers dance upon the tide,
Nature's secret, where wonders hide.

Beneath the surface, stories lie,
Of moonlit nights and stars up high.
Each ripple tells a tale untold,
Of timeless magic, brave and bold.

The willow bows, in quiet grace,
As breezes weave through time and space.
Reflections shimmer, hearts embrace,
In stillness found, a sacred place.

So pause a while, let silence reign,
In depths of peace, release the pain.
Enchanted waters hum their song,
Where every spirit feels it’s strong.

Dawn of the Enchanted Heart

Awake, the dawn whispers anew,
With golden light, the world will strew.
In shadows released from their plight,
The heart ignites with pure delight.

Beneath the trees, soft breezes flow,
Awakening dreams tucked deep below.
The sun greets life with tender care,
A promise of joy spun through the air.

In the morning glow, possibilities rise,
Each breath a chance, a sweet surprise.
The enchanted heart beats bold and free,
In nature's grasp, it longs to be.

Let love unfold with each new light,
A dance that twirls from day to night.
With every heartbeat, magic starts,
In the dawn's embrace, we find our parts.

The Celestial Whisperer

In the still of night, a voice does stir,
With gentle tones, it calls, it purrs.
The stars align, each twinkle bright,
A whisper woven through the night.

The cosmos hums a tale untold,
Of lovers lost and daring bold.
Each note a promise, a wish, a dream,
As stardust flows in softest stream.

A tapestry spun of light and dark,
The universe sings, igniting the spark.
Through endless skies, the echoes roam,
To every heart, they call it home.

So listen close, for moments rare,
In celestial threads, feel the care.
The whisperer speaks in silent grace,
Uniting souls in the vast embrace.

A Realm Adrift in Magic

In twilight realms where shadows play,
A magic stirs, in soft array.
Where fairies dance on petals fair,
And dreams take flight on fragrant air.

Each corner holds a secret bright,
In every flicker, the heart ignites.
With whispers sweet from leaves so green,
A place of wonder, yet to be seen.

The moonbeams weave through branches wide,
As time stands still, in tranquil stride.
In magic's grasp, we find our way,
Through realms of night, to greet the day.

So venture forth, embrace the spell,
In worlds where mysteries dwell.
For in this realm, adrift and free,
The pulse of magic swells with glee.

Beyond the Glassy Horizon

A sail unfurls in tranquil sea,
Past the edge where dreams run free.
Whispers dance upon the tide,
In every wave, the hopes reside.

Clouds paint hues of softest red,
As sun dips low to kiss the bed.
The horizon holds a tale untold,
Of journeys bright and hearts so bold.

Stars ignite the velvet night,
Guiding hearts with gentle light.
Beyond the glassy horizon's sway,
Lies the promise of a new day.

Each breath a step in the vast unknown,
Where every spirit finds its own.
With open eyes, we chase the dawn,
Embracing life, forever drawn.

Threads of Enchantment Spun in Time.

In shadows deep, the loom reveals,
Threads of dreams, the heart it heals.
Time weaves tales both old and bright,
Each moment cloaked in purest light.

Whispers soft like morning dew,
Spin the fabric of the true.
Patterns dance in timeless grace,
A tapestry of love's embrace.

With every turn, the stories grow,
Colors blend in ebb and flow.
Underneath the stars that chime,
We are stitched in love's sweet rhyme.

So let us walk this woven way,
Through night and dawn, come what may.
For in each thread, our spirits soar,
Eternal bonds forevermore.

Whispers of Enchanted Slumber

In twilight's hush, the stars awake,
A lullaby the night will make.
Softly calling, dreams take flight,
In whispers shared beneath the night.

Moonbeams weave a silver thread,
Wrapping souls in comfort's bed.
Each sigh a journey, calm and long,
Where shadows hum a silent song.

Through petals soft, the breezes glide,
Carrying secrets, deep inside.
In every pulse, the heart will hear,
Whispers of love, tender and near.

So close your eyes, let worries drift,
In slumber's arms, the soul will lift.
For dreams await on starlit shores,
Where magic sleeps and hope restores.

Fantasia in the Moonlight

Underneath the silver glow,
A world awakens, soft and slow.
Whispers wake in shadows bright,
Dancing gently in the night.

Crickets chant their evening song,
While fireflies twirl, where hearts belong.
Misty hills and secrets vast,
Hold the magic of the past.

In every breeze, a story breathes,
Entwined in leaves of ancient trees.
A fantasia upon the land,
Where dreams unfold, like grains of sand.

So take a step in this moonlit sea,
Let go your thoughts, just let them be.
For in this realm of sighs and light,
Life's pure wonder takes its flight.

The Sorceress’s Lullaby

In shadows deep, the whispers flow,
Enchanting dreams where moonlight glows.
A soothing chant on winds of night,
Softly cradling the world in light.

Her spell weaves peace, a gentle hand,
Guiding the restless to distant land.
With every note, the stars align,
In her embrace, the hearts entwine.

The nightingale sings, a soft refrain,
Echoing through the silken rain.
Peace descends like autumn leaves,
In the realm where magic breathes.

Close your eyes, let worries cease,
For in her lullaby, find your peace.
Dream of wonders, vast and wide,
In the sorceress’s love abide.

Starlit Reveries

Under the cloak of midnight skies,
Whispers of stars slowly rise.
Dreams take flight on silver wings,
Each moment a joy that starlight brings.

In the stillness, stories weave,
Of lovers lost and hearts that cleave.
Beneath the celestial ballet bright,
We dance with shadows, lost in light.

Velvet nights with secrets deep,
The cosmos guards what we keep.
In every twinkle, past meets new,
Holding promises, pure and true.

Awakened souls in reverie,
Bound by the stars' sweet, timeless decree.
As we drift on this endless sea,
In starlit dreams, together we're free.

Threads of a Celestial Tapestry

Woven in night's embrace so tight,
Threads of starlight, bold and bright.
Constellations dance, a cosmic play,
Patterns of dreams in grand array.

Each string a tale of time and fate,
Crafted by hands that weave and create.
Silver and gold in intricate spins,
Binding the universe as it begins.

Galaxies twist in vibrant hues,
Painting the darkness with mystic views.
Among these threads, our stories flow,
Unraveled destinies begin to glow.

In the loom of night, we find our place,
Interwoven tales of love and grace.
Among the stars, we seek and share,
In this tapestry, forever care.

Moonbeams and Mischief

The moonlit whispers call the night,
With twinkling eyes, a playful sight.
Among the shadows, laughter plays,
Dancing in mischief's gentle haze.

Fairies scamper through silver beams,
Adventurers lost in secret dreams.
Chasing echoes of ghostly sounds,
In a world where whimsy abounds.

Every corner holds a secret plot,
As shadows weave with the moonlit dot.
Darkened paths serenade the bold,
In this night where stories unfold.

So let the laughter fill the air,
In moonbeams glimmer, free from care.
Embrace the magic, never flee,
For mischief reigns, wild and free.

Captured by the Fable

In twilight's embrace, tales unfold,
Whispers of secrets, dreams retold.
Mysterious shadows dance in the night,
Echoes of stories take vibrant flight.

Woven with magic, every thread bright,
Spinning old legends, with hope in sight.
Captured in fables, heartbeats align,
Lost in a world where wonders entwine.

Voices of ancients, calling my name,
Under the starlight, we play their game.
Each page turned brings a spark of grace,
Time slips away in this timeless place.

Through pages of wonder, my spirit soars,
Beyond the horizon, the adventure roars.
Captured by fables, I'll never grow old,
In tales and dreams, life's magic is bold.

Wandering Through Illusion

In a realm where nothing is real,
I wander through dreams with curious zeal.
Mirrors reflect what the heart desires,
Flames of the mind spark endless fires.

Shadows whisper secrets untold,
Colors that shimmer, too vivid, too bold.
Step by step, I drift and glide,
Caught in a moment where worlds collide.

Illusions shimmer like stars in the sea,
Truth dances lightly, elusive and free.
With every heartbeat, I lose my way,
Wandering the veils where fantasies play.

Fleeting like mist, the visions will fade,
Yet in the illusion, my spirit is laid.
Forever enchanted by sights that deceive,
In wandering dreams, I choose to believe.

Ballet of the Ethereal Lights

Twinkling stars in a velvet sky,
Whirling in harmony, they dance up high.
A ballet unfolds on the canvas of night,
As ethereal lights set the world alight.

Glittering pathways of shimmering dreams,
Each twirl and leap, as vibrant as beams.
The moon bows low to the spirit's flight,
In this cosmic theater, all feels so right.

A symphony crafted in whispers and sighs,
As comets and fireflies drift through the skies.
The stars shimmer softly, a delicate hue,
In the ballet of lights, I find my true view.

With each fleeting moment, the magic ignites,
As shadows embrace, lost in their flights.
A dance of the cosmos, so grand and divine,
In the ballet of lights, our hearts intertwine.

The Sorcery of Sleep

Cradled in twilight, my eyelids grow heavy,
The sorcery whispers, the night is ready.
A lullaby beckons from shadows nearby,
In the realm of slumber, where dreams learn to fly.

Softly it pulls me through clouds made of silk,
Where rivers of stardust flow smooth as milk.
Wrapped in the comfort of night's sweet embrace,
Time melts away in this magical space.

Night creatures gather, their stories unfold,
In patches of darkness, where wonders are gold.
The sorcery of sleep, a gentle decree,
Unlocks hidden realms deep inside me.

With each breath I take, I drift further still,
As whispers of dreams fill the air with a thrill.
The sorcery lingers, enchanting my mind,
In the haven of dreams, true peace I will find.

Echoes from the Dreamforge

In shadows deep, where whispers play,
The dreamers weave by night and day.
With silent thoughts they shape and mold,
A tapestry of dreams retold.

In corners bright, the visions spring,
From fleeting glances, hopes take wing.
A spark ignites, a fire starts,
As echoes dance in longing hearts.

With gentle hands, they craft their fate,
In twilight's haze, they contemplate.
Each dream a door, each wish a key,
Unlocking realms for hearts set free.

When dawn arrives, the dreams take flight,
As whispers fade into the light.
Yet in the forge, the echoes stay,
A symphony of night and day.

Serenade of the Starlit Lake

Beneath the sky where starlight gleams,
A serenade flows with gentle dreams.
By water's edge, the shadows sway,
As night unfolds in soft ballet.

The moonlight dances on the waves,
In quiet grace, the heart behaves.
With every ripple, love's refrain,
A timeless song that calls again.

Whispers of water, secrets told,
In every drop, a wish of gold.
Reflections shimmer, hopes awake,
In night's embrace, the starlit lake.

As breezes hum and branches lean,
The world rests softly, calm and serene.
The melody of dreams takes flight,
In harmony beneath the night.

The Alchemist's Slumber

In chambers dim, he finds his rest,
The alchemist sleeps, dreams manifest.
With whispered spells, the night unfolds,
A world where transformation holds.

Within his mind, the elements swirl,
Gold from lead, as fates unfurl.
Each fleeting thought, a recipe rare,
In slumber's grasp, he crafts with care.

The stars are ink, the moon his pen,
He writes of magic again and again.
In dreams he brews a fragrant potion,
A dance of dreams, a wild notion.

When morning wakes, the spells shall break,
Yet in his heart, they won't forsake.
With every dawn, the promise stays,
Of alchemical nights and golden days.

Celestial Dances at Dusk

As day descends, the heavens glow,
Celestial beings start their show.
With graceful steps and gentle sighs,
In twilight's arms, the magic lies.

Stars begin their playful sway,
In cosmic waltz, they glide away.
A whispering breeze, a soft caress,
As night unveils its starry dress.

The universe joins in one great song,
In harmony, they all belong.
A tapestry of light and lore,
A dance of dreams forevermore.

As shadows merge and twilight fades,
The stars align in serenades.
With every heartbeat, night proceeds,
In celestial dances, the spirit feeds.

A Sojourn Through Illusion

In shadows deep, the whispers glide,
Where truth and fantasy collide.
A tapestry of silk and thread,
With visions woven, dreams are fed.

A path unseen, a winding maze,
In twilight's glow, we drift and gaze.
Each step a dance, a fleeting chance,
Within the realm of firefly romance.

The heart beats soft, a gentle tune,
Beneath the watchful silver moon.
With every breath, the world expands,
A fleeting grasp of time in hands.

We chase the phantoms, lost and free,
In the embrace of memory.
Let go of chains that bind the mind,
In whispers, dreams and hopes unwind.

Spirits of the Lustrous Night

Beneath the stars, they softly sway,
The spirits dance in night’s array.
With laughter ringing through the air,
They weave their magic, light as prayer.

In shadows deep, their forms take flight,
Illuminated by starlit white.
They guide the lonely, the dreamers bold,
With stories whispered, ages old.

The moonlit path begins to sing,
Of secret realms and fleeting spring.
With every twirl, they paint the sky,
In colors that never fade or die.

So close your eyes, let spirits soar,
In the embrace of night’s soft lore.
With every heartbeat, magic grows,
In dreams of wonder, the night bestows.

Kaleidoscope of Dreams

Through shifting colors, visions blend,
In kaleidoscope, beginnings mend.
A dance of hues, both bright and rare,
Where stories linger in the air.

Moments flash, a transient glow,
Whispers carried by breezes low.
In fragments of light, we find release,
A symphony of soft, sweet peace.

With open hearts, we touch the sky,
As echoes of hope begin to fly.
In every turn, the world we see,
Is painted with our reverie.

In dreams we wander, hand in hand,
Across a vibrant, shifting land.
Each thought a petal, soft and bright,
In kaleidoscope of endless light.

Touching the Essence of Whimsy

With every tick, the clock unwinds,
In realms of whimsy, joy finds minds.
A sprinkle of laughter, a dash of play,
In the soft embrace of a bright ballet.

Curlicues swirl, as shadows laugh,
In nonsensical tunes, we chase our path.
The world turns round in a splendid spree,
Where reality bends, and spirits are free.

A feathered hat, a crooked grin,
In this delightful dance, we spin.
The essence of joy, in colors bright,
With every heartbeat, we ignite the night.

So take my hand, let's skip along,
To the melody of our playful song.
In a world where whimsy leads the way,
We'll touch the essence of a bright new day.

Visions Beneath the Veil

In shadows deep, where whispers dwell,
Dreams unfold, their stories swell.
Mysteries wrapped in silken lace,
Secrets linger in this hidden space.

Time cascades like autumn leaves,
The heart believes what it perceives.
Light and dark entwined in grace,
Visions pulse in quiet place.

Beyond the veil, the world is spun,
Each thread a tale, some lost, some won.
Glimmers dance on edges bright,
Through the shadows, they ignite.

In dreams we find the paths we missed,
A fleeting touch, a whispered kiss.
Beneath the veil, we seek and yearn,
For every flame, a spark to burn.

Starlit Visions

Under a dome of midnight skies,
Wishes soar, like fireflies.
Constellations weave their lore,
Each twinkle hints of tales galore.

With every breath, the cosmos sings,
Infinite dreams on silken wings.
A galaxy of thoughts align,
In starlit visions, hearts combine.

Whispers from the moonlight's thread,
Guiding dreams where few have tread.
The night unfolds its canvas wide,
In starlit visions, hope resides.

We paint our dreams with silver beams,
In vaulted nights, we chase our dreams.
For every star, a wish we cast,
In starlit visions, forever last.

The Enigma of a Bewitched Night

Beneath the canopy of sighs,
An enigma in the midnight lies.
Echoes linger in the cool,
Where shadows dance, they often fool.

A flicker here, a ghostly trace,
Mystery wrapped in the night's embrace.
Soft spells woven in the air,
The bewitched night holds secrets rare.

Faint melodies whispering low,
Draw us closer, to the glow.
In every heartbeat, magic swirls,
Creating worlds where time unfurls.

Captured moments, fleeting bright,
In the enigma of the night.
For every shadow, there's a light,
In dreams that dance till morning's flight.

Invocation of the Nightingale

In twilight hours, the nightingale,
Sings sweetly soft, a tender tale.
Her voice a thread through dusky air,
An invocation, pure and rare.

With every note, the stars awake,
A symphony, as dawn will break.
Each call a longing, every sigh,
In the heart's depth, spirits fly.

The woods embrace her serenade,
In shadows where the dreams cascade.
Awake the echoes, pure delight,
With every song, the world ignites.

In the enchantment, we find our place,
The nightingale brings warmth and grace.
An invocation, soft and bright,
Guiding us through the velvet night.

Canvas of an Otherworld

Colors blur beneath the sky,
A tapestry of dreams does lie,
Winding paths of ethereal grace,
In shadowed realms, we find our place.

Glimmers of light, a whispered song,
Where time and space, together, throng,
Brushstrokes dance on a twilight seam,
A canvas woven from every dream.

Voices call from the canvassed mist,
In every hue, a soul's subsist,
In silence ripe with radiant hues,
We paint the world with vibrant views.

Beyond the veil, where spirits dwell,
The tales of lives, they weave and tell,
Each stroke a journey, each color a flight,
On the canvas, they ignite the night.

Glistening Secrets of the Celestials

Stars cascade in the velvet dark,
Each with a secret, each a spark,
Whispers carried on cosmic winds,
In starlit realms, our journey begins.

Glistening eyes of the ancient skies,
Guard dreams and hopes that never die,
Celestial bodies in endless dance,
A ballet of fate, a timeless romance.

Nebulas bloom in vibrant throng,
Such beauty sings to the night so long,
Each memory woven in silver threads,
Glistening secrets; our hearts it spreads.

In the quiet, a melody plays,
Of the universe, a cosmic praise,
A tapestry woven from dreams of old,
In celestial light, our souls unfold.

Crystals and Phantoms in Twilight

Shadows flicker where the light fades,
Crystals shimmer in twilight's glades,
Echoes of whispers in the cool air,
Phantoms dance without a care.

Reflections caught in fractured glass,
Time lingers here, moments pass,
Each crystal holds a story's thread,
Of love and loss, of dreams long dead.

Twilight drapes a velvet cloak,
As haunting melodies softly stoke,
The flames of memory, lost yet near,
In this fading light, they reappear.

In the silence, tales unfold,
Of magic new and legends old,
Crystals weep in the dark's embrace,
Phantoms whisper, a ghostly trace.

The Spellbound Heart

In a garden where wildflowers bloom,
A spell is cast in the soft perfume,
Whispers of magic in petals bright,
With every heartbeat, the day turns night.

The moonlight weaves through branches bare,
Casting shadows, a lover's lair,
With every breath, a promise found,
In the spellbound heart, a love profound.

Embers glow in the silent dim,
Where time stands still on a fragile whim,
Souls entwined with a gentle grace,
In the magic's hold, we find our place.

Laughter dances on the evening breeze,
In a world of wonder, hearts find ease,
The spell is cast, forever tight,
In the spark of love, we take our flight.

Melodies of the Moonlit Pond

Whispers dance on silver waves,
Reflecting dreams of secret caves,
Night's embrace holds softest sighs,
Beneath the quilt of starlit skies.

Crickets sing a gentle tune,
While fireflies flicker, bright as June,
The water's surface, calm and clear,
Carries stories for all to hear.

In shadows deep, the willows sway,
Guarding the magic of the bay,
Ripples shimmer, hearts align,
In this tranquil world, divine.

Lost in time, the night expands,
All is perfect, just as planned,
In moonlit waters, dreams arise,
In harmony, the spirit flies.

Flickers of the Enchanted

In twilight's glow, the sparkles gleam,
A world awash in every dream,
Petals dance with fragrant grace,
While echoes trace the hidden space.

Beneath the boughs where shadows play,
Moonlit whispers guide the way,
Every flicker, every sound,
A tapestry of magic found.

Mysteries swirl in evening air,
A symphony beyond compare,
Stars cascade like gentle rain,
Illuminating joy and pain.

Fables weave through branches high,
As laughter stirs the night sky,
In enchanted realms where dreams ignite,
Each flicker glows, they shine so bright.

Pathways of Stardust

Through cosmic trails where wonders meet,
The universe whispers soft and sweet,
Stars twinkle like a mirthful choir,
Guiding souls to their heart's desire.

Nebulae swirl in colors bold,
Tales of lovers and legends told,
Every path, a story spun,
Under the gaze of the eternal sun.

Galaxies twirl in a timeless dance,
Encouraging all to take a chance,
With every step, the stardust glows,
Igniting sparks as the journey flows.

In the vast expanse, we find our place,
Connected by energy, love, and grace,
With pathways bright, colliding fates,
In stardust dreams, our destiny waits.

The Enchanted Elysium

In meadows rich with blooms so fair,
The fragrance swirls upon the air,
A paradise where spirits roam,
In the heart of nature's home.

Rays of sunlight kiss the earth,
Celebrating life and rebirth,
Every creature, every song,
In this realm where we belong.

Mountains rise, eternally strong,
Guarding secrets, ancient and long,
Rivers flow with stories true,
Whispering magic to me and you.

In Elysium, love reigns supreme,
Where hope ignites each cherished dream,
A haven bright, a sacred space,
In the enchanted, we find our grace.

Milton Keynes UK
Ingram Content Group UK Ltd.
UKHW030750121124
451094UK00013B/801